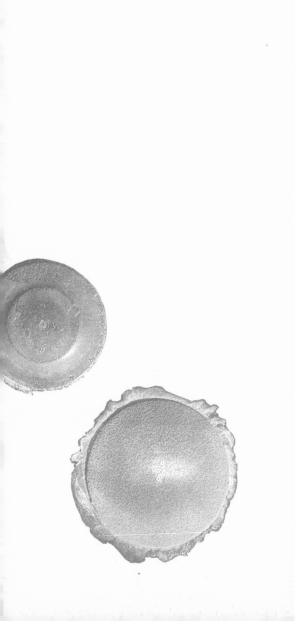

The Lease

Mathew Henderson

Coach House Books | Toronto

first edition

Published with the generous assistance of the Canada Council for the Arts and the Ontario Arts Council. Coach House also acknowledges the support of the Government of Canada through the Canada Book Fund and the Government of Ontario through the Ontario Book Publishing Tax Credit.

This is a work of fiction. Any resemblance to persons living or dead is purely coincidental.

LIBRARY AND ARCHIVES CANADA CATALOGUING IN PUBLICATION

Henderson, Matthew, 1985–
    The Lease / Matthew Henderson.

ISBN 978-1-55245-263-9

I. Title.

PS8615.E525L43 2012   C811'.6   C2012-904680-9

The Lease is available as an ebook: ISBN 978 1 77056 322 3.

THE RANCH

You sleep on stacked mattresses and mice run
the floor, biting at toes; you wake, set traps
and stack the mattresses higher still.
This is old Sask summer: flax and mustard
paint the horizon the bright yellow colour of sun
you find in children's pictures, and always
the sky is just another dead prairie above you.

Everything you remember lives inside
the chicken-farm homestead
with its back-broken frame and that reek
of old water sitting still. At night the house breathes
with open windows, swells at the seams.
At sunrise, it exhales a dust so fine
you think of bull hearts, dried and ground.

When it's gutted of furniture, you find imprints
in the carpet: four beds, two dressers, a shelf.
And from those years when no one kept it,
from before the oil and the oilmen came, the mark
where the deer walked in, lay down and died.

.

FENCELESS

There are no signposts, no old men waiting
to tell you *here*. This place repeats itself;
everywhere you've been is folded into grass
and dirt, and you blame chance, not science,
for putting the iron here, like no seismic charts
were read, no holes drilled, as if wealthy men
and god just wanted you sweating in the mud.

But the cows, they can find borders even under
daylight's sterile sun, watch nations grow
from boot prints, divide the plain by men
and else. They graze away, uncountable,
unheard as you walk the field, tool to tool,
with no sense of what is yours, and what is not.

At midnight, under the shelter of the flare,
everything is smaller; the world flits in firelight;
cows gather in darkness near the edge of the site,
scratching thighs against steel tankers.
Gut sounds and groans fill the lease like Braille.
Coyote howls leap over each other in the stark
beyond your sight. The flow and whistle of the well
quiets, and your world, the flare, begins to shrink.
You feel your stomach tighten, a dirty man
at a tundra fire, wrapped in leather,
chewing meat, a thousand years ago.

THE TANK

Squats three days at a time in white-brown mud
that sticks and sucks, like a mouth, against
everything it touches. The long battle,
the bit-by-bit of urging steel to the centre
of the earth. You dream of sinking, past
the slow riot of oil, sand and stone,
to the bottom of the prairie shield.

Rig out. The pylons packed, extinguishers
strapped, the guy wires of the stack, plucked,
swing loose again against the sky. Everything ends,
briefly, and the iron world moves on.

Only the tire ruts are left, six inches
deep, wet with water and an oil sheen,
and even these are eaten over by wheat
and flax and mustard seeds.

No mark survives this place: you too will yield
to unmemory. Give everything you are
in three-day pieces. Watch the gypsy iron
move, follow its commands.
Tend the rusted steel like a shepherd.

Across the field you can see a farm girl who might be pretty,
stripped down and out of her father's coveralls.
Might get you hard if she wasn't hidden so well.
Kinda gets you hard anyway, as she climbs the tractor,
her legs bouncing against the sides of her loose rubber boots.
Remember where you came from? What the girls were like there?
Now open the fucking well and walk the pipe like a healer,
your ungloved palm hovering over the unions.

She's in the tractor now, over there, radio on,
windows cracked, texting a guy from school while you hit
the first sandoff of the day – ball frack, zone two,
and Bill tells you, *Right now, down below, there's enough nitrogen,*
sand and shit to shoot one of those fat fuck thousand-pounders
from TV right the fuck out of his bed, so open that bastard slow.

And then, *Nevermind*, and he does it himself.
The thin pipe rattles, your lightest pipe, the stuff you solo
around the lease on your shoulder. The whole line kicks
and, standing beside the flowback tank, the noise is older
than anything you've ever heard, like you've always been hearing it,
and just now became aware. The first time you drove a car
the engine kicked, sounded like a coil cleanout,
a blowdown, a frack, a bleedoff. When you learned to
knead dough, your father's palms over your hands,
there was a man outside punching holes in the earth,
making your mother's windows buzz and rattle.
Does the farm girl hear this, over there,
in the tractor cab? Does she know it's you?

Near the end where the steel turns ninety degrees,
goes straight up, some burr inside catches, peels off,
and the sand cuts through the pipe and into the air.
But your hands, they're already in an X above your head,
when you remember the sign for *shut the fucking well.*

FIRST DAY

Everyone can tell that you're a virgin,
that when your shot came, you were too full
of rum to do anything but bully your dick
into a condom and watch it cower.
And when Rachel said, *Fuck me*, you didn't,
couldn't, but shucked the Trojan to the floor
of Brian's cottage where the girls would
find it later, make you go and pick it up.

They know all right. They see it in the way
you wrench, the way you tie your boots,
but they say nothing, hammering harder
and harder, sounding off for you
the hundreds they've taken to bed.

BUBBLES

They called him Bubbles before you met him,
flat-ass in the dirt working a snare, legs spread
like a child's to catch and hold a rolling ball.
A man from a world without children,
he had no soft voice inside him.
He confessed it in every word, with a mouth
that knew only wood and steel, brick and earth.

His wooden hands grew into whatever tools
he touched. The day he recoloured the lease:
twelve hours of wordless painting
in prairie heat so heavy he was caught by it
like an insect trapped in the brush's path,
licked into the colour of the pipe.
At shift's end, you knew nothing about him,
but when you heard his name, pictured fresh red paint.

He kept one eye on a gopher hole,
closed the other to keep from blinking.
After an hour, stood suddenly with a struggling twine,
the noosed gopher scratching at air
as if the thickness of it might help him scramble out.
When he asked you what to do you spit seeds,
said, *Retard. Eat it, fuck off.*

Into the field until his arms go taut,
he stops, something looses inside him
and he swings the twine against the ground.
Five times, ten, until the string goes limp.
Rodent chirps on the first, and the second.
But by the third, there are already no sounds.

WHO ARE YOU OUT THERE?

The rig is between the derrick and the tongs,
and the mouths still dry from last night's whiskey
and this morning's dirt. They trip like it's all they know,
like tanned gears sweating beside each other.
This lasts forever, this rigging, this tripping.

You're no part of it. You can only watch
as they throw tongs and catch string like conversation,
watch steel slip into earth sixty feet at a time.
Tilt your head to see the swab line buck and spray,
and feel everything as the oil turns your face brown.

FRIENDLY ADVICE

Asking for push-slaps, regardless what your supervisor tells you,
will get you nothing but the imprint of the push's hand on your face.

There is no such thing as a pipe stretcher, and all thumb wrenches
are left-handed – and there are no thumb wrenches west of NFLD.

Your hardhat did not come with a 'whee' in it, but a truck driver
will still remove one for you by throwing it across lease, yelling *whee*.

Do not calibrate the shivs: your arms will tire of being thrown up into
the air, your legs will ache from kicking off the ground, and your ass

will hurt from sitting on a bucket in thirty below while everyone laughs
at you. Under no circumstance should you contact the labour board.

But, a few months from now, when a new guy shows up, way greener
than you, do what it takes to make him look as stupid as you can.

STEVEN

Loves his kids, hates their moms. Wears wife-beaters
like someone slapped a paintbrush down his chest,
left him stained, white-striped and dirty. His belly
seems swollen, reaches from his skinny frame so that
when he falls into a chair he looks, always, like he's been
feasting. All he eats are 7-Eleven frozens, heated and rushed
to his mouth on plastic, he breaks the cardboard flat
at the corners, licks it clean. Steven will tell you
he ran with gangs in Calgary and has some Native in him:
Everyone from Sask does. His truck blares Corb Lund;
he brings you whiskey in a coffee pot to drink as he drives.

YOU ASK YOUR FATHER WHAT A LEASE IS

And he tells you about the geese beyond
the aqueduct, how they turn the sky grey,
how as a teen he never put his gun away dirty.
You remember the blue steel cleaner,
the sound of a rag drawn through a barrel,
and still, you catch the scent of solvent rising
from buried cells that ruled you as a boy.

The lease is meaningless: a square paced
first by seismic workers, and then your father,
and then by every other man you know.
But you've always pulled meaning from nothing,
and when he leads you to an empty field you
tear grass in fistfuls, read the roots like a will.

ON DRIVING, WAITING AND KILLING

You learn, after a few trips,
how the engine shaking down
into the tires brings gophers
peeking from their holes.

And you learned, after the pile
of red and soft and little nails
grew larger, that no matter
how hard your earth shakes,
that even if reality starts to fall
in pieces to the floor, you can't go
looking for answers, can't give
yourself to the boy and the rifle
who are waiting for your head.

MIGRANT

I

You see bats, owls, palm-sized moths, all backlit
by the flare, known by their shadows, the little hairs
or feathers or dirty white dust that shingles their wings.
The pipeline hisses around you, cools under a white
frost that grows thick even in the unsunned swelter
of the night. You grip the line like a throat, squeeze
until water falls down your forearm, your fingers ache.

II

The oil moves from hand to face, your skin painted
pale brown, dusted dark with dirt and seeds. Smaller
hands once grasped at trees instead of steel, and sap
stuck your fingers closed, was wiped into your eyes
until the lids caught and balked with every blink.
You broke branches, kicked old trunks until they bled
dead matter, spilled their secrets to ground in larval letters.

III

The forest fell away before you, and grew thick behind.
That place knew itself even in darkness, when all the earth
and animals were what you named them. Where you climbed,
wild. Pines stretched upward and down at once, unkempt
branches twisting like roots toward the sky. You pissed where
you pleased, carried an axe on your shoulder like a man; if it fell
wrong there would be no one to sew you shut or carry you home.

IV

There is earth below your earth, a deep room where
gas and oil, rock and stone, circulate like slow blood
through a body. The world beyond the flare,
the up-close of prairie grass in the dark: beetles and mice,
haggard coyotes who lie on their backs, face the sky
like it's a mother, wait to be fed. The spotlights show moths,
a billion beating wings that make the air so thick and dark
you can't even make a fist without crushing dusty bodies.

V

At three a.m. there is no world but what's contained
by the flare's domed light. A great dark glass over
an insect; you are the only thing with feet and hands
on a flat and dying moon. A man trapped twelve hours
in the caves of the opened land with no one
searching for him, no one to know he's gone.

VI

Through the opaque air of the prairie night you see fire
in the distance, and beneath it men like you are still
so unlike you. They measure air in decks, fluid in metres,
count the hours till daylight on a whiteboard wall.
Because you are the only one who sees it, even the sky
is yours. In time you could turn the clouds to vortex,
cover the stars in oil, bury them underground,
feel them pulsing below like bright, electric hearts.

VII

No fish swim the barren sloughs, made worthless
by cowshit for almost anything but cows.
You see foxes now and then, hanging their heads
to tongue the tepid drops, but you catch them, later,
retching rabbit from their stomachs in the field.
And even this water brings your mind to trout:
the first one you caught, slapped down, scales on sink,
and cut, still gulping, from belly to tail. Your fingers
probing like your father's, hard against the gentle insides,
and finally the quiet as you felt a little salamander, still living,
wriggle his head free of the guts. Placed him gently
on the lawn, found him frozen the next morning.

VIII

When the push-gasp rhythm of the Texsteam dies,
you imagine the oil growing thicker in the line.
You break the pump like you're shelling fruit,
find the aching gasket, the broken diaphragm.
You change old pieces for new metal,
plastic-wrapped parts, fresh lungs in their boxes:
small and glinting, breathing shallow in and out.

IX

In the streets of Toronto gas lines rise like organs,
break ground and hang from the body. No one sees
the pumps, the regulators that live tucked in alleyways.
No one hears the migrant gas, barely hissing metres
below their feet. But you walk like a child, head down,
searching after the hum beneath the city. A mongrel,
hoping the sound will lead you to its home, take in a stray.

X

In the blank-faced hotels of the roadside prairie
you lie wrapped in floral sheets, dream of women
with tiny names planting clover in your sink.
You work the patch at night, sleep through the day.
Heat the room with your skin, boil moisture
from the air. You wake at noon and count money,
check your phone, imagine a figure bent over a desk
writing you letters, someone old and beautiful who still
knows, remembers and cares where in the world you are.

RIG IN

The sweat in August drenches your tan clothes brown;
by January it crisps your eyebrows in ice
and you fight the wind for breath.
You lay pipe like limbs along the lease,
hard shapes, hollow and straight,
they charm oil like a snake from the earth.

You do not understand this. It is not math or language,
not the migratory pattern of geese to be charted.
This is muscle lust, fucking with your eyes closed,
the body's quiet genius. You cannot map it: the elbow
twist, wrist snap, wrench tug. You give up
history, science, all the words you know in French.
Forget to watch your hands move.

At night, you ache with work ground
into muscle, bleed it out in sleep:
your arms push and pull at the air above
your bed, miming the rig in. You will wake
to steel-burred, dirty sheets, darkness,
and the diesel rumble of a new day in the drive.

RENAY

In the field Renay wore a pink bra, and the zipper
on her coveralls bounced just below her belly button.
In the office she was leggings, work boots and tight shirts.
You bitched, and you carried her pipe, stared at her tits
and imagined her, sweaty and quiet, smoothing your skin
like bed sheets with her hands. At the bar, they ate shots
of whiskey from between her legs, and you watched,
trying to be a man who thinks of a girlfriend and not Renay.
Until Jared's big right hand, the broken one, just two fingers
and a thumb, grabs your hair, drives your chin to her thighs.
Then the whiskey sting as the glass tears your lip,
your watering eyes and Renay dabbing blood from her skirt.

REMEMBER CHARLIE

In the back room of the shop you spend
a day with WHMIS and Piper Alpha
and a videotape of Charlie, burned up.
When, someday, you want to roll up
the sleeves of your coveralls, let your
bare wrists touch the breeze, risk the gas
in the air, they want you to remember him,
how he pulls his red sweater up his arms
and how you will always see his pale skin
as darker and redder than the yawning
mouths of the dogs who terrorized your youth.

The video finishes, the VCR gears click,
the tape rewinds for the next guy,
and you start guessing at appearance fees,
video royalties. Later, you and the boys
will bargain in skin percentage, trade burns
or breaks, bulk-sell fingers for a better deal.
You all figure you'd cook half your body,
the lower half, for an even million.

When Joel's wife shows up for his paycheque
a few weeks later, and when you watch
the half-circle, barrel-edged nub of his wrist
forget itself and grasp for a beer, you find
yourself tuned to every clash of steel on steel,
you see snakes shedding skin in hospital beds,
you remember Charlie, and you begin to wait.

All men must be clean shaven, a small moustache is acceptable
but the rubber has to seal. Here, your pale-boy face is a virtue;
the men dull ten razors a month. You're lazy, don't lift much
and can barely hammer, but you can stay under air for hours.
The steady in-and-out sound of oxygen rushing your face
through its tubes, that urgency of gases, forever escaping itself.
Even sour gas, heavier than air, hurries to the earth. Your supe
watches you, thirty feet away, waiting for you to drop,
and you think of how the gas can kill your lungs, your brain,
but your ears, they're fine, your fingers, fine. And could it get
into your coveralls, sneak up inside your ass, finish you that way.
Incident report: fatality, worker dies from H_2S-anus contact.
All employees must wear latex underwear, bums must be clean
shaven. A little hair is acceptable, but the rubber has to seal.

BIRTHDAY

You noticed you were older somewhere in Alberta,
felt your back turn eighteen while you pulled
at the hatches on the tank. A shift like you must
have felt before, but with your arms already flexing
against the day you couldn't help but notice that you grew.
On your second birthday you found your hands,
on your third, your voice; at thirteen you knew your dick
and balls, what they had been waiting for; and now
you hear something awaken inside you, like the birdsong
of childhood, noises you could never quite identify.

Sparrow, somewhere south near the old barn,
the end point in a line drawn by your father's pointing hand.
Blue Jay, above you in the limbs, always above,
sounding faintly like baseball. And *Teal*, whose voice
surrounded you on the wharf at seven, as you watched
a gudgeon lie flat on the wood, gulping.

It seems like strength you're hearing, tendons snapping
into place, and you begin working to the rhythm,
twisting your torso like you'd never had a body before.
Behind you, the supervisors stand in a weak circle
on a dusking prairie, listen to the vac truck revving up,
watch you work. Not one of them sees youth growing
jealous inside you, the violence of puberty still tucked
into the bend of your elbow, the angle of your spine,
the silence of the lease as you drag the sledge,
watching their skulls open and close at the mouth.

DAN

Is a father and a husband, an oilman and a cowboy,
but says he's hung up his husbanding boots for good.
Forgets you're lazy when you get poker on the work PC.
There's no bar where he's not comfortable, no place
with liquor he will not dance. Cowboy hat bobbing
in a crowd of metalheads, boots shuffling through
the forgetfulness of the two-step. He has a look, the hang
of his cheeks, that tells the pierced-up kids around him
that his boots have broken ribs. And while his toes dance
in circles, you know that if a man were to snatch his hat,
playful like or angry, he'd beat him right to fucking death.

OILFIELD LOVE POEM

Town is his wife. His daughter: Elizabeth.
Out here is just pussy: shower, shave,
condoms, call home, *Goodnight I love you.*

You hear big hands on the door,
the sway of the housekeeping sign.
Listen with closed eyes to the quiet,
liquored fucking one bed over.

You hear the wake-up call, an engine
choked from sleep, the whistle of the gas
and the night shift pulling up. His phone:
Goodnight, I love you. And you love her too,
like she's the last woman not in the patch.

DRILLERS

A few hundred metres of staked grass and grit,
it takes two days just to move their iron in.
Awkward as they settle, their arms hanging,
like they know how pointless they are next to
the hydraulics, to the conviction it takes to move
a village like this. Maybe a roughneck grabs
a wrench, cleans a truck or hauls some shit
from here to there, but mostly they just watch
the rig rise up around them. The shacks come
to hold the engineers, the college kids who lie
inside on bare beds, listening to the steel whimper
and grind into place. And while they unroll
their sleeping bags, another fifty men, centuries ago,
lie on their bellies in the dirt, crawling closer year
by year, waiting to overtake you in your sleep.

ON FITS AND BLEEDING

Because you are a child, and an idiot,
and because you see in yourself a significance
that is not there, you wait till two a.m., when,
alone at the tank, you get dramatic and try to
punch yourself in the head. You think of the kid
you called a retard in school, how he blackened
his own eye, and if you're better than this place,
then why is this place so hard.

But you bitch out at the last second,
catch the rim of your hardhat, and open
a line across your knuckles. You say you fell,
and he sees the rim of your lid, barely red,
the blood on the clipboard, the toe of your boot,
but shuts up, drops you at the hotel in the morning.
And there will be no woman waiting in your room
to dab you with her shirt, lick your fist until it scars.

TODD

Fat, slow and one hell of a guy, a year ago
it took four boys to hold his legs
while he did kegstands on grad night.
He's slow, heavier than anything else on lease,
and the lease, you have to tell him,
is just where you work. No, *Where you work
is the lease*. Confusing because it isn't beer
or smokes or a car stereo system.
You watch him uncap a downward-facing pipe
and crane his neck low and to the left
as the heavy gas falls through the fingers
on his porkchop hand. He grabs at the air
and, each time he opens his fist,
looks disappointed to see how he's failed,
again, to catch what you said would be sky
the colour of oil on a summer puddle.

COWS AT NIGHT

They lick air like salt, shoulder to flank,
groaning forward. Ripples in the darkness,
shapeless, if not for the rodeo memories,
the flicker of the flare along their backs.

This is when you think of meat and leather,
as if there is nothing else to say of a thousand legs,
haunching through shadows like cornfields.
As if every question still left inside the night
must be broken into currency, counted.

SERVICE RIG

Half these men are boys, like you are, but yell
so loud the cracks in their voices are hard to catch.
The other half, giants, older than the rig itself,
they knew this oil before it was black. A bare chest
here is thin and folded into itself a thousand times.

You've never seen them take the head off the pumpjack,
it's clean in the dirt when you arrive, but you get to see
the service rig rising, the tongs turn on. Watch the youngest
man on crew climb the derrick and stand, harnessed,
coveralls dropped from his chest and tied with the sleeves
around his waist. Up where no one can yell at him to zip up,
no one can tell him to remember Charlie, where he can feel
the prairie wind beating his chest like the skinny fists
of a woman who almost wants him to let her go.

BADLANDS

Your father worked Drumheller while you ate and slept at home.
He travelled the badlands, squatted below rocks, read books
you never knew he read. He sat until his eyes strained to know
what the prairie insisted he must see. Once he found a hoodoo,
toppled after centuries of reaching beyond the flattened earth
we all become and remembering that, once, it was a mountain.
He stripped naked and coated himself with spit and dirt,
arched his back into the rocks and let his speckled shoulders
fade under mud, until his whole body became that colour.
When he dressed himself again, jeans over earth-caked legs,
he walked back to the lease, and danced and prayed for the well to flow.
Your father worked Drumheller while you ate and slept at home,
he stalked the badlands with his shotgun and a pack of smokes.

WAKEUP

This morning begins at three p.m. You don't shower,
the grease of last night's work already collected
around the hotel drain. They sell gum in the lobby,
your fifth pack this week. Just in case she touches
your hand as she takes the cash, in case she wants
your story, in case she wants to tell you hers.

By five, you're in the truck. Chuck kicks the clutch,
you can't drive stick, cuts onto the highway
with Sirius rock and dirty talk-radio blaring.
He tells you he had a coke problem,
but you learn that's not a problem at all.

You barely speak, there are so few things now
that could happen to one of you and not both.
Tonight will be twelve hours, plus two driving.
There were twelve days like this in the last fifteen.
A hundred eighty-two hours by the end of the night;
you don't see lovers this often. You don't see lovers.

Halfway there, you start to like the drive,
find deer outside your window in the heat and the air.
And though their novelty has faded, you feel skin
in the leather under your forearm, the snap of muscles
contracting, burred fur. Like they're leading you
to the lease, as if you could be led anywhere else.

SELF-PORTRAIT IN OIL

You gauge the flowback, and the dipstick
sends your reflection swirling, bouncing
through the fluid to the steel sides of the tank,
back to when your mother's arms could hold
you still and clip your nails. Could hike you
over puddles by your collar, stronger
than anything else you knew, you still
feel her hands sifting through your hair
for lice when you clean with bleach;
the smell of toil and tiled floors trapped
in the creases of her skin. But now you're
here, and your own arms, your hands,
overnight, have grown bigger, rougher,
than you ever wanted them to be,
and you can hike no collars of your own
without strangling the neck beneath.

AT NIGHT

The sixty-metre walk from office trailer
to well, to tank, and back again, lasts longer
than the ninth and tenth grades combined.
And like the night that senior girl, Sarah,
kissed you, vodka and licorice, you won't talk
about this place, you won't ever be sure it's real.

In these minutes, each night, you can move skies,
open holes in the earth to stare at the oil sea below
as it once was: a writhing tide of hooves and fur,
of horses kicking off the backs beneath them,
desperate, certain that if they could just grip you
in their maws, reality would rattle from their bones.

PENTHOUSE LETTERS

Some oilman wrote in about his driller, secret love,
and when the laughter stopped, no one made a gay joke
or pretended to grab the derrickhand's dick for a month
and a half. And when they couldn't bear it anymore,
when all the pretending that there were no cocks on the lease
was too much to take, the ass-grabbing started again.

KELSEY

This girl was supposed to be Steven's.
When, after a few drinks, she starts kissing you,
he tells you to fuck off and leaves but comes back later,
while she's pissing, and asks if you will share.

Just home for the summer, she's suspicious:
thinks the green-bound Heaney is your way of tricking
girls into bed. After two months in this motel room,
it's stranger to see someone touching your things
than to feel her fingers curl against your shoulder,
on the left side where the muscles tore
when Steven dropped his end of the pipe.

A ballplayer, hardball, national level.
You wish she would believe you really just want to talk,
and kiss a little and, if she wants her body felt,
or if she wants to touch your dick that's fine,
but you mostly just want to talk.

She says her school is down in Texas, Christian too,
but she goes there more for baseball than Jesus.
They won't let boys inside her dorm and maybe
that's why she has to leave so fast when you take her hand
in your palm and press them both against your crotch.

You wonder if you can get out before her, lock the door
behind you, and run home to her house, fall asleep in her bed.
You will wake to bacon and eggs, a family breakfast
where everyone mistakes you for Kelsey.

You will cuddle with her sisters and they'll pretend
you aren't half-hard against their backs. Her father
will kiss your forehead, call you *darling* and help you
practice pitching in the backyard. And a lifetime behind
you, a girl paces the motel room, pulls strips of callus
from her heels, scalds her hands in the bathroom sink.
Sits with her back against the door before turning
and chipping half her fingernails on the knob,
anything to try and wake her from your life.

WHAT HANDS DO

Two hours to the iron, they stare at the road
but do not speak. Hands don't speak,
don't eat or sleep either. They lift and hammer,
mark oil in and oil out. They wade through gas
that sits thick as wet wool inside your lungs.

Hands scrub trucks, rack pipe and paint bins,
follow the boss like dogs. He tells stories
and they listen: how his father died last fall,
how thin those palms became. Listen and nod,
wring oil from the earth. They do not speak.

SINKING PLACES

You're just a kid, still afraid of fire
and, though you do it every day, the panic
you feel before opening the well never fades.
When you see the gauge at 30 MPA,
you become a cat bound in cotton strips,
wrench your body, gnaw your snare-strapped
veins. Your face works toward the only corpse
you've ever seen: unafraid, indestructible.

But you remember being this man, this man
who, on his first time kicking down in water,
found nothing, but calmed his limbs enough
to sink with grace. You wait, the two of you,
for a hand or hook to pull you from this place.

A GOOD DAY

There are those days of sunlight,
when the smell of gasoline mixes
with your grandfather's garden,
when life feels better than good enough.
You play at happiness with worn
technique: windows down, music,
wind and a grin you only half
need to remember to wear.

Your aching is an inventory of the way
the earth has changed, of the iron
bent to your will, the wills of men
who will you. On these days,
you keep a piece of yourself for hoping.
As if hope alone could tend the ocean,
could hold it above you just a while
more before it crushes the record
clean, ravines the prairie and scrubs
the sum of your summers to
bent steel beams, cracked alfalfa.

NEWS

While the Hutterite roughnecks trip
pipe you sit in the shack and read
about the London Tube bombings,
listen to the steel singing down into
the well. The paper says there is a prince
at Suffield Base, he spends his leave
at Cowboys asking after panty colours
and leaving twenties on the table.

The prairie bristles, jealous you still
know, still dream of other lands.
While your head is down, the flat earth
curls up at the edges, crests like a wave
that will never crash. You fall from the door
and your shout is drowned as the diesel
rig roar crawls up and out of your chest.

DAVE TALKS ABOUT 'THIS ONE GUY'

This one guy, this one guy was on lease,
the frackers failed their pressure test,
and the line split and he wasn't anywhere near it.
Nowhere near it. And yeah, so it could separate your legs
from your body, but that's why he wasn't anywhere
fucking near it, see, and that's why it's a test. Right.
It's called a test. But this guy quits. Really.
He goes and gets himself a shrink who gets him on comp
because he had a *traumatic experience*. Like a soldier,
like, from fucking Iraq. But all those airgunners from Lakeside,
you know, they wake up screaming most fucking nights.
No shit they do, and then they go back to work the next day
and they kill themselves a hundred more cows.
And you remember that day, when we were out there
and the oil carried over, shot out the stack
and the whole lease went up? And you and I, we stood
at the tank and we fucking *worked*, in *that*, with all that fire
behind us. And yeah, you pissed yourself: so what?
You pissed yourself because you didn't have a choice,
because that's what work *is*, right?

BILL

A badger dead against the range road
on the day you met, flattened and spreading
its marshy smell across the prairie. Bill said
they're rare here, and for a moment the scent
turned the grain to muddy water,
covering generations of birds and rodents, trapping the waft
of their losing bodies beneath you. For years
you thought of Bill as being connected to dead animals
while he thought of you as lucky. When his daughter
took ill he found an old Indian to give him feathers,
tied them to the mirror of his truck.
He talked about guardians, animal guides, spirits
who came to him in dreams. The doctors took
a piece of her brain and the house
filled with incense. He held her tight,
old women pressed her forehead with their hands
and murmured. He grew sunflowers six feet tall
and dried their faces, floated them in raspberry wine
beneath her bed until she found her balance.
At work he measured twice, checked salinity again
and again, straightened every line of pipe
on lease and hammered them almost too tight,
as if a seizure could leak from any crack,
cover all the sunflowers and raspberries,
choke the world with dark black mud.

You can see the smoke by Vauxhall.
A short day, a shallow frack.
You reach home, but keep driving,
through Brooks, past the patch motels,
to Newell and its oil-smudged sky.

As a child you painted your face this colour,
ash from driftwood burnt on the beach,
jellyfish drifting upside down, charting
dead angles, the sand against your stings.

A blowout, they both guess: Mike in back,
kingcab, and the supe driving. It's all sour too.
You hit a barricade a kilometre out, Firemaster
trucks everywhere, the campground evacuated.

Two dead when the stabbing valve went,
the pipe swung so fast it took one guy's face
clean off. But you only know this later.
On that day, you drive with your asses
off the leather, so close to yourselves,
toes curling after something solid,
a foothold inside your steel-toed boots.

UNCLE AND THE FAT MAN

They call the skinny one Uncle, you forget
the fat one's name at the end of every shift.
They crack Pilsners on the morning ride
home, a twelve-pack in forty minutes,
the bottles smashed under road signs
all the way from work to Weyburn.

When they laugh, or speak, or slap down
hard against your back, you remember
that you could come up behind them napping,
leaning back in office chairs, and cut
their necks to show them, their families,
show the ones who think you're tender, the ones
who love you, show everyone who doubts
it, who you really are, who you've always been.

BREAKUP

Men lose their trucks in April, cave by May
and pump gas at ten an hour. The snow melts,
the earth soaks to mud too thick for rigs to move.

The sky is a leaky roof and they dream of catching
rain in buckets. Cocaine turns to codeine.
Cash bleeds out like a well. Their clothes stink,
they eat the dollar menu, bitch about road bans.

Some even go to Lakeside, work the killing floor,
shave beef from bodies hung on hooks and belts.
Run the gun. Avoid the eyes. The single-filed flesh
of thousands sluices through the grated floor.
All until the sun batters the earth to grit again.

VULCAN, AB

Today, there is only one bar on this planet,
and inside it Renay crosses and uncrosses her legs.
All of her panties are at home or upstairs
in the hotel room she has all to herself.
The jukebox is digital, the future today,
and it plays Crüe and AC/DC all night long.
Your supe rocks Deer Hunter with a stranger,
tosses his glass to the floor when he tags a doe.

When you're drunk enough, and by yourself,
you break a knuckle in the bathroom.
And though the cut on your fist closes over,
and your bruised elbows pale with time,
the wall above the urinal, where for a moment
you forgot who you were, might have kept
a crust of blood, a scrape of skin between its tiles,
might remember you by them, even now.

DEVIN

He blares porn to prove he's not gay. He drinks
at cross-shift, and you watch a goose stalk
the ranch, loose down falling from her breast.
You kid at killing her, but it's still only July.

All geese love deeply, black or grey or white.
If left alone, she'd march the yard, heartsick,
shedding fat and feathers till you found her dead,
eyelids creeping in like tarps pulled over ice.

But he fired from the hip while you slept.
After the bragging, a nest. Held her eggs
in your hands, touched them to your cheek,
your ear, as if the hearts inside could speak,
beat hard enough, loud enough, to reach you.

WHORE TO YOUR DOOR

They slip flyers under every windshield wiper,
on every truck, at every hotel in town.
There is always coke, his or hers.
Sometimes he snorts so much he can't get hard,
so she just talks to him, tells him
everything's fine. It's a different kind of lie,
but that's all he really wanted anyway.

Her finger is stained with gloss the colour
of her lips, and her heart's not gold,
but made of papier-mâché, a Grade 3
origami crane folded flat inside her purse.
While she sits on the bed in his hotel room,
he can't curse or rough his hands along
her body, and he can't fuck her till she cries,
like he bragged to you he would. Faint music plays
from her iPod on the table, and at half past two
in the afternoon he reads the room as midnight,
her mouth a sheet pinned over the windows.

GARY

December 25th is sixty hours long: double time and a half
to let his kids call Santa *Daddy*. The wife wears Sears
diamonds under the collar of her housecoat, drinks Starbucks
homebrew, and goes barefoot all day waiting for the six p.m.
shake of a one-tonne in her driveway. The kids remember him,
mostly by his smell. If you asked them to guess, they'd say
something between Walmart packaging and the garage floor.
Some days, he comes home to silence, sits at the table
in covies or dirty jeans, feels his house surround him,
the plasma screen, doilies, angels on the wall, lets his gut fall
to his lap, waiting for someone to finally find him out.

DAVE

Says things like: *No thanks, it gets in my mouth,*
when offered strings of jerky. Self-proclaimed
hardest-working man in the patch. He brings
his dog and daughter right on through the shop,
and she doesn't even notice the shit he says,
as if the scarce little curls left on his head still say
enough about her braids to remind her he's hers.

Don't threaten me with paradise,
I was looking for a job when I found this one.
And he's still looking for something at the bottom
of his jug: lemon water and cayenne pepper
that never seems to empty though it's always
pressed against his lips. Did he sleep on the flight
back from Saudi? Could he keep his tongue in check,
surrounded by men so much darker than the Natives
who sleep, curled up, on his hometown streets?

SHITTING IN THE TREES

The land dips so slowly you can't notice the slide
that lies hidden until spring when the melt unveils a lake
that's been waiting to pour itself across an empty field.
It's like this all over. Now and then you see pine trees
in the middle of the plains, though you rarely reach them.

Once, when you needed to shit in daylight and the lease
was covered in men you walked a half-mile with a pail
and a garbage bag to a circle of trees. Inside the wood
you could almost be at home, your home. Crouched over
you nearly lost track of the hydraulic drone, the noises
of the work so faint you were left to fill in the roaring,
of drillers and company men, by memory alone.

JOE TALKS ABOUT SNUBBING

Most dangerous job in the patch, really,
I won't even do it. Clint, you know Clint,
he lost his supe on a snubjob – his first week
of fieldwork too. Clint told me the rig burned
so hot they had to pry bones from the metal –
that's a closed-casket, boy, rough service. Rough.

But yeah, it's tripping under pressure.
Basically pushing pipe down a hole
that wants to push you back. It's when
the patch itself gets so goddamn angry –

You don't remember the rest.
You can only think of Joe's elbows
on the table, dirty or freckled,
when he told you to avoid the nipple.
When he mimed lifting a breast
with four fingers on his left hand
and tilted his head, darting his tongue
in and out under the imaginary tit.

Right there, that's what they like,
just underneath. Get your tongue
in there, boys. My ex-wife, real good girl,
Christ, she giggled like fuck for that.

WHAT YOU DO

At some point you will drip oil from your glove to the ground
and think of how far this place is from real. You will watch
ten men catch gophers, paint them red and let them rip each other
apart for fear of blood. You will call women whores, measure distance
in *cunt hairs* and encourage a man to *go get him some gash.*
You will wonder if you are still Catholic enough to keep a sin,
and if these sins are sharp enough to leave you scarred.

James wants to tour Thailand. He's excited by the cheap sex,
the freedom from condoms and lube and the chance to make
a woman he does not know, cannot know for lack of language,
cry out from his roughness – or at least that's what he says, maybe
he's just afraid that one of you would reach out and hold his head
and press your forearm against the small of his back.
Or maybe he is that rare man who's exactly what he says he is.
When he talks you quease and pull away, but grow a little
more like him for all your shutting up. As if he could leak
into you with words, as if they held any power here.

IMPOSTER

When your flight lands in Toronto, you whisper
to the ground crew through the glass. You get up
and leave the plane and join their orange line.
You end up hauling baggage and dragging
the length of fuel hose to the hull, its awkward
push-pull weight reminding you of how badly
we all both need and fear to couple. With face mask
and goggles frosted over like the rest of your
body, they can't even tell you've come from some
other herd. It isn't until later, in the staff showers,
when you're wet and naked, that they drop their towels,
their soap and half-zipped jeans, and move forward
all at once. The last thing you will know is the stink
of jet fuel and body wash before you're eaten alive.

CAITLIN

You're long gone by now, but you hear
that there's a baby coming and flashback
to hugging her, chests together, hips apart.
The most you ever touched, but for a second
you wanted to fuck her; maybe wondered
more than wanted. You worry the kid
is yours; it seems like enough that you
stripped her down in your mind, down to
the desperate teen you thought you were
too good to want. It seemed real enough
to leave a kid behind. And there she is,
in this prairie house, away from anyone
who knows you both, and inside her
stomach, a flesh about to kick.
And is it feet and hands that grow in her,
or something as lustful and sad as empty
as its father and the way that it was made.

SOMEDAY

You will lie about these men,
cut their rounded edges straight,
stretch their lives to simple violence.
Each brother you hated,
every father you found,
you turn them over in the end.

And you will make yourself apart,
as if you were ever more than trying,
than faking, lurking. As if, still tethered
to the womb, you didn't just conjure
each of them with that first and hungry
gasp you let slip into the world.
As if you've ever stopped your howling.

ACKNOWLEDGEMENTS

I owe much to Kevin Connolly for his generous advice and critical mind, to Al Moritz and Richard Lemm for being talented and kind mentors, and to the entire faculty of the Guelph MFA programme and the UPEI English Department.

Thanks to my friends Paul, Jake and Elisabeth, who have never failed to offer criticism, advice or encouragement, no matter how suddenly they were needed. And to the many others who have shown me interest, encouragement or kindness.

And thank you, especially, to Hillary, without whom I would manage very, very little.

Some poems from this collection previously appeared in *Descant, Misunderstandings Magazine, Maisonneuve,* Toronto Poetry Vendors and *The Walrus.*

I am very grateful to the Ontario Arts Council for their generous support.

ABOUT THE AUTHOR

Mathew Henderson is a recent grad of the University of Guelph's MFA program. Originally from Prince Edward Island, he now lives in Toronto, writes about the prairies and teaches at Humber College.

He has had poems published by Toronto Poetry Vendors and *Misunderstandings Magazine*, and has work appearing in future issues of *Descant* and *Maison-neuve*. *The Lease* is his first book.

Typeset in Roos.

Printed in August 2012 at the old Coach House on bpNichol Lane in Toronto, Ontario, on Zephyr Antique Laid paper, which was manufactured, acid-free, in Saint-Jérôme, Quebec, from second-growth forests. This book was printed with vegetable-based ink on a 1965 Heidelberg kord offset litho press. Its pages were folded on a Baumfolder, gathered by hand, bound on a Sulby Auto-Minabinda and trimmed on a Polar single-knife cutter.

Edited by Kevin Connolly
Designed by Evan Munday
Cover images by Michael Chase
Author photograph by Hillary Rexe

Coach House Books
80 bpNichol Lane
Toronto ON M5S 3J4
Canada

416 979 2217
800 367 6360

mail@chbooks.com
www.chbooks.com